JUSTIN SANE -
THE JOY
AND PAIN
OF A
BEAUTIFUL
MAN'S SOUL

JUSTIN SANE -
THE JOY AND PAIN
OF A
BEAUTIFUL MAN'S SOUL

A Dance with Addiction and Mental Health

Justin P. Dodson

To order additional copies of this book, contact:
Xlibris
844-714-8691
www.Xlibris.com
Orders@Xlibris.com
819778

CONTENTS

HOPE

MIND DREAMS

HIGHER LOVE

ONE LOVE

SOUL LOVE

Dedication

One Love
Love to Live and Live to Love

These are words by my son, Justin "Googles" Dodson. The writings and art are reflections of some of his blessings and curses. Being an addict and bipolar did by no means define him. He truly wanted to share himself, help the broken, and help people understand the daily battle. He loved all who reached out to him. He did not achieve his dream of publishing a book before passing away from an overdose. But with his guiding presence, many angels, and by the Holy Spirit, we have created a book from his love.

Until we meet at the sun,
Mom

Blessed Are the Broken

The soul cannot bend to the force of time. It is affected by our grease and grime. Faith is in the eye of the beholder; it is quick to crush like a boulder.

Whatever opens your eyes to see, do not question why. Just let it be. The heart and the mind can be tricky tools and can lose you like a treasure of jewels. The broken in life are the truly blessed. They are given a quest to solve the test.

Pain and Joy

My life has been like the experience of drugs. I have had the most overwhelming rush of euphoria that your body could ever endure. I am a master of pain and pleasure in life. And to balance out the equilibrium of the body, you must undergo an immense amount of torture on your body as you come down from the drugs. You go from the highest of highs to the lowest of lows, all sometimes within an hour. This is insane on your body, mind, and soul. This is why I am the way I am. Using the roller coaster metaphor does not do justice to the truth that I attempt to explain.

My writing may come off as dark, and it would be easy to diagnose me as a depressed individual who lives with suicidal ideations on a regular basis. Thankfully though, I am bipolar, so I can live on both sides of the coin. I am a very happy guy, and I have learned to love myself, the good and the bad. My problems are the things I cannot change and have control over. I find that I must write of the horrors in my life in order for me to accept my place in the world. I have also learned not to hold things in and not to lie to myself. I understand that I may be too brutally honest, and I apologize to my loved ones. I'm an asshole, but if I wasn't, I would be dead. Transferring emotions like pain and fear into something tangible, such as words, helps me connect the dots. It helps me change my perspective of a situation and make a positive out of a negative. From extreme lows to extreme highs, acceptance gives this awesome wave of relaxation that brings a smile to my face and a tear to the eye.

Pain and joy are both my weaknesses and my strengths. Maybe my pleasure experiences are more personal than my sad ones. Maybe I'm embarrassed at what I find joy in. Maybe I don't want to glorify the life of addiction and mental health. Or maybe I don't want to turn a positive into a negative. All I know is good triumphs evil no matter how much balance is needed. My life has given me more joy than pain, and the overflow from both leave streaks of tears down my face. My life has been a constant cycle of birth and death along with a continuously changing perspective of pain and joy.

SECTION 1

Owning It

Psychoanalysis of Myself

My entire existence has been full of *Uppers, Downers, and All Arounders*. This is a book I read in a PSU health class, and it's a perfect life title. It feels like I've been to every extremity of the world and mind. I'm clinically bipolar, but I think it has a lot to do with how I treat my body and how I perceive personal experiences. I was often alone playing as a child, then boom, family birthday party with twenty loving people all around me. My family was everything; you could say I got a high from the situation. I now know that statement is entirely true, front and back. The seasonal death of a relative or loved one was very difficult to bear over and over. I did not understand death and fought it in the worst possible way. I was never told that I can control the way I perceive an event. I can make it as good or as bad as I want. I did not know this; I am still very challenged with controlling my emotions. I wanted to know the answer to everything as a child, and I never stopped questioning. This is both a gift and a curse. Having a question for everything is just as bad as having a worry for everything. It drives you mad. I realized that I received this power from my gram. Over time, "why" has made me become an angry person. The answers were not always acceptable, and I would get angry at why.

Uppers, Downers, and All Arounders. Along with leading a bipolar life, I have also come to terms that I had split personalities. Nothing extreme, although it had still made an impact on my life. I had too many questions to stick with one personality; you must diversify in order to get all the answers. This granted me the power of lie and manipulation. Having multiple personalities confuses who you are inside. I've lost myself in a maze of *whys*. I found that it's easier to control multiple lives instead of just one. I'm not sure if this is true for everyone or just the special few. My soul remains consistent and wise; however, my heart and mind are very erratic.

I am able to look at someone I know and deeply feel inside me what they are going through. I feel empathy for others to the maximum degree, and this is greatly troubling. Some hallucinogens give the mind this ability, and it really can give you a deep love and respect for those around you. This is why these drugs are used in many spiritual rituals around the world and have been for all time. I've always had a feel for others, and I'm confident that I could have a connection with whomever I desire. I've made friends with many criminals over the years, ranging everywhere on the scale. I found out most of them were good people inside. Empathy has taught me how to deal with others better, and that led me to better understand myself. It gives me the desire to help others. Others' concerns have always been a project for me, because this kept the focus off me. Listening to others is a very underrated idea in the world today. Listening leads to trust, which leads the person to acceptance regardless of whether or not my opinions are right or wrong. I always possessed the power of giving my perceptions to others in assisting them with their problems and concerns. I get a high from helping others.

Uppers, Downers, and All Arounders. I've seen the full spectrum of life, and I've learned to embrace everything in a more enlightened mood. I realize I have the control of how good or bad I perceive the situation, no matter how traumatic the event. Asking why has kept me entertained and alive, and I appreciate both. It put me ahead, and it led to exploring more in the playground of life. I know who or what my soul is even if I don't know who I am. This has been proven. Knowing how to communicate with others is essential in the existence of mankind. Being able to feel another person's emotions is a serial experience. It gives you a bond with the person that you will never forget. It creates love, and love is all we will ever need. The equilibrium of life must be full of good, bad, and ugly. It is the life there has always been, just in individualized perceptions. If you know what you are going into, it makes you a lot more comfortable, which is usually a good thing. Evolution takes time and purpose. Use your physical and psychological environment to stimulate asking why. The power of now is all we have control over, and this will shed light on the folds of time. Use everything to grow: everything includes many shades. Smile, it can all be fun. Open *up* your mind, set *down* your fears, and it can *all around* be a good time.

Early Drug History

A long time ago, I thought I was a big man in a small world. I always hung out with people a year ahead of me. One day they asked if I wanted to smoke some weed, and this was the start of some bad decision-making, partly to fit in and partly because I'm a curious person. It felt like I was walking on the moon; I loved the feeling. However, I noticed that when I smoked at parties, I would be too weirded out to be social, and I didn't like that aspect. So I decided to drink instead. I was always an intelligent person, so I never had to work very hard throughout school, which made it seem like I was a healthy clean kid. Mom had no idea that I was partying all the time. I managed to be able to balance fun and work, and everything was great. I'm naturally a social person, but that is not always a good trait. I talked with everyone around and knew everything that was happening.

In ninth grade, all my older friends went to high school, which scared the shit outta me 'cause I thought I'd be all alone. But that was the best year of my life. The new friends I made are the ones I'm still with today. Well, some of them. I still basically stuck with drinking, but we had so much fun just being immature. As the year went on, I gradually started smoking more and more. It was more about fucking around than getting fucked up.

I hit high school and had a blast. The partying was now every weekend, but smoking was starting to be daily. Girls tried starting relationships, and I would go along until a party came up. I was an all-American boy growing up and was athletic enough to play most sports. Unfortunately, drug testing began in high school, and I just could not stop the partying. So I played intramural sports instead of team sports.

In junior year, Mom started having concerns and placed me in a drug and alcohol program at school. I was pissed at first but soon realized it gave me an excuse to get out of class and talk to friends about drugs. I tried pills, but I mainly stuck to weed and alcohol. Some of my friends started shooting dope, and I was totally against it. It pissed me off and saddened me. I did what I could to help them stop, and for a while, there was hope. I wasn't about to give up; they were family, and I learned to accept things. People getting fucked up became my normal. Needless to say, curiosity killed the cat. My plan was to try it once...I loved the feeling. That made me stop caring what people thought before there was an issue, at least that was what I told myself.

My senior year, I partied every day and could still do well in my classes. I could control how often I used dope. My friend started selling, and I reaped the benefits; until next thing I knew, he was in jail. I cleaned up my act, but I began to drink heavily instead. And I gradually tried to control dope again and again; insanity became a daily friend and foe. Dope was ruining my life, and everyone knew it. I was late for Christmas dinner because I had to get high to eat. This fucking disgusted me. I finally had enough and was accepted in a Suboxone treatment plan. However, I could not stop everything, so I went to rehab to stay in treatment. It took me way too long to realize that the world is a hell of a lot bigger than I thought.

Rehab Life

War is seen in the eyes of many. Blood drips down into pools of tears. Dreams are a continuous playback of tortuous movies from the hell of life. Days are full of depression and existence.

I was told that drug and alcohol rehabs would change me into a better man—that my struggles and life would be lighter and my addictive personality could be controlled and a new self would be born.

My experiences in rehabs, and there's been a few, have been quite interesting, similar, and a world of fun. The first step is the detoxification. History of drug and medical illnesses are assessed, and then you are given a bed, which will be your resting spot for several days. Don't let this sound like sleeping beauty time because by no means is the body and mind at rest. Exercise is bathroom trips to hug the toilet, sit on the throne, or lie on the tile.

There are times you have a roommate and get to share their hell. Between snoring and bathroom breaks, you do get the glorious moment of sleep. But then the nightmare starts over and over again. The mind is in full fear and does not know how to escape.

Medication is given to help as you go through the most intense chemical storm of your life. From the war, I developed a seizure disorder.

I learned a lot in rehabs—the good, the bad, and the ugly.

Everything in life is a seed that is planted. Some will grow, and some will not. Some take longer to grow than others. From my advantage point now, I see baby seedlings and grandfather-sized oak trees. You have to look to see life; otherwise you will be stumbling along the desert lost for all eternity.

Willpower

It is crazy how one pill can make or break your entire day. It can kill or save you, legal or illegal. If a heroin addict does not have the drug induced into their system, they will undergo severe physical trauma. Symptoms will be high temperature, high pulse rate, and high blood pressure. Death will be welcomed in the next week or two.

Sleep comes in spurts of minutes, and when awake, the body is covered in sweat. Nausea is then the first sensation felt. Food is not a possibility, and dehydration is inevitable. This is physical and not in the same ballpark as the psychological madness. The mind runs to safety and comfort, just as the addict. This will come when the pain decreases.

Anything and nothing works—hot bath, cold shower, cigarette, water, hold stomach, throw up, shit, stare at the TV, or move to bed, to chair, to floor. The brain cannot concentrate, and conversation is difficult. You want no one around, but you crave help at the same time. Pure hell. The mind is the only prison cell that you cannot escape.

If a gun was present, suicide would be welcomed. Bold. True. I wouldn't wish it on my worst enemy. The sickest torture is this will happen over and over. There are three options: suicide; try and keep well, keeping daily intake of the dope; or quit. This is what every addict wants to achieve.

It is the hardest job for anyone to overcome and maintain. It's asking to give their best friend and lover to another man. In my mind, it's like Jesus, nailed to the cross until you bleed out three days later. Then going to hell and being raped by the devil. Finally, rising again to tell your glorious story. You must survive each day knowing that it could all happen again and again.

Jesus is great, and he suffered the addicts' sin, pain, and agony to heal us. Bold. True. I *am* Justin Dodson, and I'm a recovering addict. I will pray for you.

Now

Life situation is mind stuff; life is real and is now.
Allow is isness of all things.
Is there joy, ease, and lightness in what I am doing?
If no, change how or what you are doing.
Am I at ease at this moment? What's going on inside me at this moment?
Now gives power to do anything.
Complaining makes you the victim—take action or speak out to get power.
To change your here and now.

Three choices: remove yourself, change it, or accept it totally.
Acceptance = surrender = freedom.
It's as good as it gets now—free now.
"Sorry to keep you waiting." "It's okay. I wasn't waiting. Just here enjoying myself."
In joy of myself.
Outer journey may be a million steps—inner journey has only one.
That step is now.
What's my next thought going to be? Long pause = intense presence and highly alert.
God said, "I am that I am." No time (past-future), just presence.
Jesus became Christ because of presence.
On second coming of Jesus, he said, "I am truth. I am divine presence. I am eternal life. I am within you. I am here. I am now."
Don't depend on groups or teachers for presence; depend on yourself.
Makes you free from sin.
Space of objects = space of thoughts.
Space = silence = stillness.
If there was no illusion, there would be no enlightenment.

The luminous splendor of the colorless light of emptiness—own true self.

Every addiction arises from an unconscious refusal to face and move through your own pain.

Main challenge:

Male—thinking mind

Female—pain body

Efficiency

I have spent my whole life taking the easy way out. I thought I was just being efficient and being smart. I've realized now that this is a terrible way to go about. It made me into a sluggish person who waits till the last minute to throw something together. Oddly, it usually turns out pretty good.

The little bits of stress have built up over the years, and I'm ready to explode. I struggle in life because you have to teach yourself and manage your own time. My track record doesn't speak highly of time management. Half-assing is just putting off work till later. It's like continuing to stay well with dope instead of biting the bullet and quitting. I've been putting off issues from the past, and now I'm being hit with issues from years ago. Everything is so overwhelming. I can't control feelings and emotions.

Quitting drugs is one thing, but processing traumatic events in my life is too much with a clear conscience. I'm kicking myself for having to deal with all this stress right now. Being efficient doesn't fly in recovery. The process is slow, and it is seemingly impossible for an addict's mentality. We want what we want, and we want it now.

Slow and steady and hard work is against our religion. This is why most fail—too many hurdles in a row, the distance of a marathon. We are treated like children because of our mentality, but even children know the slow and steady turtle wins the race.

Be proud of all accomplishments and understand that you must crawl before you can walk, you must walk before you can run, and you must practice before you can race.

If you fall, get back on your feet. Even Jesus fell three times. All good things don't come easy in life. You've definitely been to hell, but the stairway to heaven is right before your eyes.

SECTION 2

Different Perspective

I Try

Half of the time I feel invincible to death. Half of the time I pray for the escape of death. And half of the time I am quite dead to the world. I don't know which half-filled glass to choose each day. Having no fear to die comes at the price of having no fear to live. Love and hate have a lot more hope than nothing at all. I don't forget most dreams; I forget most days. Each day I try for the glass half-full.

Seasonal Depression

One snowy morning, I found myself in a frustratingly difficult automobile complexity. I was hungover and had to change my flat tire my friend accidentally popped the night before. My hands were iced up because I had no gloves while I was working with the frozen metal objects. My girlfriend sat inside nice and toasty with a warming smile.

This is a normal situation during the winter months of the north. Time appears to freeze for the days the sun is lost. Daylight savings is set to destroy humanity. It gives society less dimmed light to work with each day. We lose sun, heat, joy, and freedom. It makes people formulate strange choices. Not getting enough sun deplete many vitamins and minerals. Vampires are sexy, but they are scary as well. Being trapped indoors for the winter causes some people seasonal depression. The outdoors, woods, trees, and sun disappear, which is even worse to a chronically depressed individual. Even under the perfect daily tale butterflies and sun-glistening days with virgin princesses in every forest, us mentally challenged may be full of despair. Even we depressed can say, "I'm sorry. I need to lie in bed and feel like death for a few days. But tell the princess to wait, and I promise I will get to her."

So snow plus less sun equals vampires. Most can walk in the gray winter light, but they never look the same as from their photos. Some quench on the thirst of alcohol to feed on their hunger of me to stay warm in their new sweaters. Men get their bonuses too. No need to shave or cut hair, and they can wear the same hoodies. Our fat is hidden under our hair and baggy clothes. This thus transforms the once vampires into real-life zombies. Eat, drink, and consume. They look down on you for taking a nap instead of getting drunk, getting fat, and spending money. I'm positive the dream that I don't remember from last night beats out the windy, freezing cold. What winter really does to people is force us to either find ourselves or distract ourselves until the return of the sun.

We all need distractions in one form or another. Some may be healthy, and some are not. Anything repetitive for days and hours at a time is a problem. For addicts, the walls fall in and your dreams become worse. Past thoughts come back years later, but everything seems like it was better then. Flashbacks from anything traumatic can appear over and over. People read, pray, sleep, drink, drug, or work more than moderation. The scales tip; and relationships, suppressed emotions, and the health of society come at a price. The world is set this way to prey on innocent victims. They want us to drink more around our loved ones so we can just forget all over again. They want us to give all our money to the church so we can buy our way into heaven. They want us to buy love with expensive gifts so we can be more in debt. They don't just want these things from us; they need for us to do this—for America. Sometimes you have to fake a conversation with your cousin so you're not out cold on the porch. Freedom is not found with or out of a set of boundaries. Just don't make freedom your misery as well. Stay warm.

Inner Goodness

The saints of the world must sacrifice their lives for the devil as much as God. I have heard lost souls and broken tears. I have heard the dreams of murderers, and I have heard the cries of the innocent.

I left a party to go get high with my best friend. We snuck inside his parents' house to get the supplies that we needed and proceeded with our business. Quickly we were finished and on our way back. The streets went by, as I was high. I reached the destination to the show before it was even known. My boy overdosed in my front seat. My friends were terrified and didn't know what to say. I just got in my car and pointed on the way. I got my friend to the hospital just in time, as the doctors said. I did as much as he did. I saved him, leaving, not realizing the magnification of the situation. I did my senior project on heroin, and I gave my class a speech about a different friend but similar overdose story. They were speechless.

My friends have come to me and told me about being raped. These are people I know and people I love. I never thought that I would know murderers, rape victims, and everyone to the fullest. I have heard stories that will forever alter my existence. I take no pride in gathering all these tears. I do take pride in the tears that I have shared with these people.

Throughout the search for the truth in this world, I realize that there is entirely too much pain. Everyone has it, everyone hides it, everyone throws it in your face, and everyone has pride in it. But behind every story is the storytellers' eyes. This is where the truth is held. Feel the pain that is shining through their eyes. That is when you feel the story and not just hear it. If you keep searching through the eyes, you will find the inner goodness crying out for help. You can see their innocence, their reasoning, and their true self. Not the ego proud war story. I've met a lot of bad people, I've met a lot of good people whom bad things had happened to, and I've experienced many bad things myself. But behind every story I felt and not just heard, I could see the inner peace through their eyes. Everyone has good in them. Take pride in that.

Hide and Go Seek

I know what it feels like to rather throw up than look in the mirror,
When the phone rings for days but you dare not answer because of fear,
When there are faces all around but no one is near.
You need to be reborn.
You need to be reborn.
You can't start over, but you can change the difficulty to easy.
Wake up from your nightmare and stop being crazy.
Get off your ass and stop being lazy.

When you're in the darkness with eerie sounds all around, no one can save you from your deepest fears. Night and day go by, but you can never see the light. It seems as if the hands of time have stopped and the realm of existence has been torn apart. You need to be reborn. You have to do more than just find yourself. You must find yourself, hold the light, and maintain your happiness day by day. This process is difficult and strenuous, but it is definitely achievable by all. You must first want to change. This is more than acceptance; this is true desire for a change. The inspiration can come from anywhere in life; it is a fire that you cannot ignore. You have to find this power within your soul in order for you to succeed.

If love alone could take people away from addiction, abuse, sorrow, and misery, there would be no pain. Unfortunately, this is not the case. Love is a key ingredient; however, most people don't feel this gift until later in the rebirth process. Forced change does not work either. All the jails, rehabs, gods, books, and meetings in the world won't affect a person who does not want it. Those resources just teach you how to lie and manipulate yourself and others into believing that you are just fine. You have to use knowledge and experience as your guidance. These things are solid, and you can't argue and fight with them as much.

Understand that your brain is your tool; it is not who you are. When you lie in bed, you can watch your mind drift to random needless thoughts. You are not controlling these thoughts but rather just observing the information as an innocent bystander. It is your subconscious at work, but you are able to take a step back and watch and learn. Your conscience can be seen too, all throughout your dreams and life. Once you see this and understand this, you can finally relax. Understand that your mind makes mistakes and can be easily corrupted by many forces. The brain can release chemicals that take away emotions, take away motor functions, and even take away the will to live. It can make you have a conversation with someone who is not even there. Once you see this, you can now use your mind as a tool in the journey of life. It also alleviates some self-blame and depression. You were not using your tools right instead of not using your life right. Any relief is welcomed, but relief that stays is recovery.

The heart is another tool that could make or break your life. We have all been torn when our heart says yes but our mind says no. Sometimes we listen to one or the other, but we should listen to both and let neither decide. Again, you must step back and take a different perspective. You can't wear your heart on a sleeve or lock it up in a box. There is balance to everything. There will always be good and bad. There must be. There is purpose to both. You can let a broken nail ruin your day, or you can turn the other cheek when someone punches you in the face. You can make it as good or as bad as you want; the choice is yours. Every time a pet is lost, the lesson of death is taught to a child. Every time a game is lost, the strength to persevere and the determination to win is improved. Every time a bell rings, an angel gets her wings.

There is good in everything; it just has to be found. The bad in life makes us keep searching. If everything were good, we would stop searching. We would stop living. During this personal inner expansion, there must be many changes made in the outer world. Difficult choices have to be up to you to make about your friends and family. You don't necessarily have to cut out the addicts, assholes, and bad people in your life. You just need to get rid of the ones who are bad for you personally— the ones who kicked you when you were down, the ones who forgot about you, and the ones who stood by and watched you rot. Some people you will want to give another chance, although be wise, considering that you have a second chance as well. Look at people from a different perspective, just as you looked at yourself.

It's harder to get away from friends than it is to get away from yourself. Realize that you are not giving up on them; you are giving yourself a chance at the light. There will only be a few loved ones who stay with you during your trials and tribulations. These people are true. Most people will be new, and that can be scary, but even the old people you will now see in a new way. Remember that it is harder to change your friends than it is to change yourself.

How Are You Doing?

People ask all the time, How are you doing? But I know that mostly they don't give a shit or even listen to my answer. It's just a habit to say and something that makes you look like a good person. All they really care about, if they are thinking about me at all, is where I am working, how good I look, and if I am staying out of trouble. If I say that I'm doing great and have been really happy, most people are usually not pleased with the answer. This is because they are not happy themselves and want to bitch about something. If you want to know how I'm doing for real, that's awesome. I will give you a genuine answer and listen to your response. If you don't give a shit, then fuck off. I can tell in the first three seconds how involved you are in the conversation.

I have wasted a lot of bullshit time with people I have no care to speak with; although I am able to speak with people I have no care for. There is a big difference. I've had intelligent, meaningful conversations with people in jail whom I never knew or talked to again. I've sat next to family and friends and wanted to pull my damn teeth out just to get away from that person.

Fortunately, people change. Some just have bad days, while others need more time to develop into a person with a heart. You're not going to remember everything about everyone. I'm terrible with names, which girls really don't like. But I remember knowing this individual and feeling that we had a connection in the past. Sometimes this happens with people you just meet. Social creatures are who we are. Sharing our souls and feeling others are how we thrive and survive. Next time you ask me how I'm doing, you better fucking mean it or I'll call your bullshit.

Drugs

I have been with God, I am God, I see God, and I'm one with God. I love God because we are all God. From taking psychedelics, I have seen the laws of physics debunked while I can feel God in every sense that I have. Not everything can be captured by words or pictures. Moments can last an instant or a lifetime.

Heroin gives me the feeling that I am in bed snuggled up to God and our sweet dreams. Cocaine turns me into Jesus, and I feel my voice should be heard by everyone. Alcohol gives me peace and war with God. Benzos take all emotions out of the situation. Things are black and white without emotions. God seems as a simple warm presence, and he just wants you to drool over his magnificence.

I have had life taken before my eyes, been blinded by my eyes, and lost souls in these eyes. I have seen God standing by my side every time I have suffered through withdrawal and the judgment for my sins as my body and mind were eroding away. Every mental collapse—such as our house fire or deaths or relapses—seemed to be godless. No matter, jail, rehab, and my worst fears…no God. In my weakest emotional state, I have no godly presence. It takes time for me to overcome and feel the oneness again.

God is not there, nor is God here; God is now. You can feel him with love, you can feel him with sports, you can feel him with music, and you can feel him with nothing. It always feels free and pure with each given moment. I can feel him now, today, just for today. I cannot express with words or pictures; it can only be felt.

It Pays

I guess I have some resentment toward my father for killing himself, although I have been more accepting of the fact and have forgiven him of his mistake. I have anger toward my daughter's mother and have accepted that I can't be the father I want to be. I also have anger that I can't control drugs and alcohol in my life.

But I realize I must surrender myself in order to succeed. I get angry how quick I pick up education at school but am slow to learn drug education.

I will have to avoid bars. I will have to avoid parties. I will have to avoid people. I will stay busy through work and family activities. I will spend more time with my daughter. I will create works of art to avoid my cravings. I will continue with counseling sessions to cleanse my palate. I will believe in prayer to deal with troubling times. I will read more to educate myself through recovery. I will branch out to church to gain strength in my faith. I will surround myself with positive people in my life who will love and support me.

No Fear

I have no fear of death. I have no worry of when or why or how. It's not in my thought process. I'm not saying I want to die, but I'm not saying that I don't want to die. I don't intend on dumb decisions, but shit happens. I have cheated the hands of death either through my own will or something far greater than myself. The chances of hitting the lotto are one in a million. Chances of cheating death are probably about the same. I've hit the lotto about ten times by now. Shit, would you rather have the money or an extra life? I bet a life most of you shitheads would take the money.

I've cashed in my continues over the years just to advance to the next level; even then though, it's not the game of my ultimate demise. When I was about ten years old, my friend and I had the brilliant idea to go tubing in the flood from the rain raging behind my house. It was about an acre of floodwater rushing through the acuity. Before we knew it, we were caught up in the current, holding on to a thin tree for survival. My friend wanted to let go of the tube, but I said no, to give it to me. Then Poseidon parted the water as my stepdad came to the rescue. He used a tree floating by to pull us out of the current and to safety. I thought it was funny, but my friend was crying. My stepdad knew that I was different then.

Life is what I am afraid of. I live in the power of now, which makes everything new and unknown. And we are all afraid of the unknown. Curiosity hasn't killed this cat. Don't focus on death. Focus on life.

SECTION 3

Broken Growth

Welcome to Jail

The bars spun all around as my eyes rolled toward the back of my head. My limbs were cuffed and shackled, but my body swayed freely back and forth. The guard spit in my face, which was the most disrespectful thing he could have done. As I laughed and stared into his eyes, I knew this wasn't going to be a pleasant evening. I was out smart-assing him, and he wasn't happy. Also, there was enough liquor in me for about five DUIs. Time came for the man to escort me to the hospital. As I stumbled along, my face was used to open the solid steel door. The backlash was coming from my tongue. As blood ran down my face, my head was slammed into a cement step, and all sound disappeared. Blood dripped from my eye, nose, mouth, wrists, and ankles.

After being stitched up and released from the hospital, I was returned to jail—unfortunately, only to find out that I was being hidden in the suicide ward for actions that took place. The ward was the darkest place of my life even though the lights were on twenty-four hours a day. I had a concussion for a month, and I still have the battle wound scars. Those cuffs and shackles saved my life. I would have killed the man. Make the best of what's around.

King Heroin

King Heroin is my shepherd, I shall always want...

These tragic words, part of a twisted rewording of the beloved 23rd Psalm, were discovered in a closed car alongside a dead heroin addict. Her death was ruled a suicide. A hookup with the car's exhaust had sent carbon monoxide fumes into her vehicle.

King Heroin is my shepherd. I shall always want. He maketh me lie down in the gutters He leadeth me into the paths of wickedness. Yea, I shall walk through the valley of poverty and fear no evil for thou, heroin is with me.

Thy needs and capsule comfort me. Thou strippest the table of groceries in the presence of my family. Thou robbeth my head from reason.

My cup of sorrow runneth over. Surely, heroin addiction shall stalk me all the days of my life, and I will dwell in the House of the Damned forever.

Jail didn't cure me. Nor did hospitalization help me for long. The doctor told my family it would have been better and indeed kinder if the person who introduced me to dope had taken a gun and blown my brains out. And I wish to God he had. How I wish it.

Unknown Author

Bodyboard

It is always the waves rolling in. Time in and time out. Everything plays its role in time—the moon, the mood, the waves, and the seasons. Time has no roll in the dice. Everything just falls in order.

I have been waiting for this wave for a torturous amount of time. I was lost in time, and I am truly grateful to have found my balance in the now. As an addict, I know very well of the extreme highs and extreme lows. My brain goes through the same war, just the drugs are no longer part of the destruction.

The war was never a fight on drugs; it was just propaganda. Drugs have no ally. The warriors of the chessboard will inevitably churn—as the moon, the waves, and the seasons. Breathe in and breathe out. Now do it without time.

Thug Life

In my young adult years, I put myself around a lot of strange places and a lot of strange faces. During one adventure, my friend was having a party where we were drinking, smoking, doing drugs, and having a good time. Then this gangsta kid from Philly started talking about some other dealer who was stepping on his toes. This kid was about sixteen, and he said he was going to shoot him and all this other crazy nonsense. No one really listened or gave a fuck, and the party continued. The next day, I met up with the other thug whom the kid was talking about. I did my business and didn't mention anything about the night before.

Two days later, the dude was dead. The sixteen-year-old shot him. He told a party full of people three days prior of his full intentions on murdering this young man. No one listened, no one cared, and no one believed that this could happen in our small community. I feel terrible that I could have said something and maybe made a difference; however; I did learn a great deal from this traumatic situation.

I discovered that there are pieces of shit who live on earth, and I do not like those kinds of people. Now some don't take it to the extent of taking another life, but they do rip the very soul out of life. These people come in every shape and color and are generally attracted to gold. I learned that people take life for granted. It made me live to the fullest and fight with the best. I think of the man sitting in prison today, and I say thanks for the lesson you fucking piece of shit.

Thanksgiving

Anger makes me complain about all that is in life and blinds me to the light that is all around. This darkens my soul and tempts my mind for an easy and quick escape from my fears and tears. I am willing to give up all to get away from this heaviness and make a deal with the evildoer himself. All this does is extend the darkness and grant me a match worth of light. This tease enforces the desire to give a piece of myself again for another match, rinse and repeat. My pain increases with each inching moment, and hope has disappeared from the shine in my eye.

Hand of Darkness

I have traversed through the darkness for an untraceable amount of time. I have felt the cold bony hand in this darkness, and it would lead me toward the warmth. This would dull my senses and release a central calm throughout my body. From time to time, there would be a dim light that shone down from above. This granted me a view of my surroundings and a new perspective of my situation. It became brighter and reflected off a thousand pairs of eyes that were directed toward me. As fast as the light appeared, it diminished and returned to the terrifying darkness. The glow of the eyes were no longer there, but their presence haunted me.

Again the hand of darkness rested on my shoulder; however, relief didn't return to my soul. Instead the warmth burned my skin and stung my eyes. The dampness of the hand was chilling to the bone, and I began to understand what was before me. I was influenced by the warmth, but the eyes were burning into my soul. This is when I turned away from the hand of darkness and realized I had to find a warm heart that could lead me to the light.

Home Free

I have just been released from prison for something I did not commit. I sat patiently sitting on my justice with nothing to hold on to but my steel bunk. Everyone wanted to know what I could get, and everyone wanted to know what they could get. It's home base for all the drug connects, and everyone meets everyone very quickly. People know your business before you know your own business.

So you get out, and it's like being religiously reborn. Everything is so very vivid, and the real world is seen with kaleidoscope eyes. I hear every little cricket and smell every rose and see colors from different spectrums and the taste of the cakes that make me large and the drinks that make me small and, of course, the touch that electrifies from my every orifice. It's a sweet bliss that I want the world to know but not have to experience the immense pain that is needed to receive the miracle.

SECTION 4

Hope

Teach or Be Taught

All people are teachers to others in one way or another, and we all have instincts to trade knowledge. Some subjects are very difficult to grasp, like theological concepts or religions. Other things are easy to spread even between different languages, things like tic-tac-toe or rock, paper, scissors. Most lessons are taught to innocent minds, and this can be very joyous and very tedious. Even the best parents don't always want to answer their children's millions of questions about life. Although at times this may be difficult, it must be done. The way that the message is delivered is often more important than the message itself. Everything can either be forced down your throat, not given to you at all, or hand-gifted.

Learning a different language is a task in and of itself, but imagine trying to learn calculus in a foreign tongue. Often at times, we hate to learn, but we search our whole life for answers. Even a master can learn from an apprentice. If you think you have mastered something completely, you have lost heart in your desire. Everything must learn to grow, including earth and God. Some will say God is perfect in every way. Yet they will say the same Almighty plagued culture of sinned creatures and then flipped sides to promise everything as long as you ask for it and speak his name. It appeared like God learned that fear is not the best method to teach. My God learns and grows every day. If he didn't, there would be no point and no heart in the desire.

Not every game has an ending, not every life has an ending, and not every god has an ending. People don't understand that we can change our beliefs, and I don't know why people don't challenge themselves, their society, and their God. Each of us is being taught something every day, and it's all in how the message is given.

All Lives Matter

We are taught to do the right thing in life. We are taught to help others in duress. We are not told that nice guys finish last. We are not told that you can have repercussions for giving assistance. I have saved a few lives during my life, but unfortunately, I may have let some slip away. Most difficult subjects we must learn on our own in life, because this is the way we teach.

Once upon a time, I had a friend who was addicted to heroin and was on the verge of suicide. I spent time with him and frequently spoke to him so that he would have some positive support in his life. One night I was with him, and he overdosed. There was another "friend" with us who decided to finish shooting his bag of the overdosing heroin before he decided to give me a hand. After failed attempts of reviving him, we decided that we had to take him to the hospital to save his life. We dragged his limp body down three flights of stairs to the "friend's" car. After all the work to get the corpse to the car, the "friend" thought that it was best if he didn't take him to the hospital because he was afraid of getting in trouble with the law. He sped off, while I ran and told the neighbor to call 911. My real friend was rushed to the hospital and brought back to life by paramedics. His mother blamed me for the situation and hasn't spoken to me since. I somehow managed to convince my friend to go to rehab, which he did and still is clean and sober. Since his rebirth and for several years later, he has not spoken to me either.

Several times in my life, I have stopped abusive boyfriends from beating their girlfriends to death. As a father, son, and human being, I am compelled to help a screaming victim. Every time, it has ended up being my fault by both the boyfriend and the girlfriend. My life hasn't been threatened, but I've been in fights and have been arrested coming to aid helpless females. I have even stopped one of my own girlfriends from injecting bad heroin; I was yelled at for a week and cheated on.

When people black out from drugs and alcohol, they do things that they would never do and will never remember. There are some instances that I will never forget, no matter how hard I try.

Doing the right thing is a brave act and is not always easy to do. I know the feeling of wanting help but not taking assistance from anyone. I'm sorry for all you people. I have not learned to run away. I have not learned that I will finish last. This nice guy ain't going anywhere. I have too many people helping me. We are more alike than different, my friends.

Halloween

I have worn a bunch of faces in a bunch of places. It is much easier to live multiple lives than it is to just live one. Sometimes it's just for fun or for a job or even to save your life. The girls at Hooters don't want to sleep with you. Salespeople are not your best friends. The authorities do not want to help you. Support is given and success is made to create deceitful people. It is like magic. We all want to believe what is not there. More importantly, we want to ignore what is actually there.

Halloween gives the magic to every innocent and evil person alike. You can change your age, culture, religion, sex, and anything your imagination can conceive. The costume is only the cover of the book; playing the part makes you the story. Don't half-ass anything in life. Just do it. Make people scream or make people laugh. If you make one person smile, then you have done your job. Infants can even accomplish this.

Rise from the dead, shed some blood, and cut off your head. Everyone wants to be someone else, so lose your face. Get that out-of-body experience we all crave. Take my face and pass it around, because I'm going to be someone lost who will never be found.

Suicidal Truths

There is only one sure way to condemn your soul for an eternity of hell. That is taking your life with your own hand. This is what religion told us in order to terrify us from pursuing the event. Once the mind is able to comprehend the concept of death, it is always a question of, When am I going to die? Having the power to take your own life is the perfect example of free will. This realization is the most powerful thing a human can possess, so they do not want us knowing about this. Only God has the ability to say when you are to die. Truth is always better than fiction. This theory that God is in control comes crashing to a halt when the person actually wants to kill themselves and they realize they can if they want to.

Everyone has thought about killing themselves at one point in life. Maybe not to the same extent, but it has crossed all our minds. And at that point of suicidal pressure, you understand that you were taught total bullshit, and you feel like you have been deceived by God. This isn't how you want to feel when you have a loaded gun to your head. Everything is running through your thoughts at this time, and your mother's emotions are not on the priority list. So a lot of poor kids kill themselves because they found out that they could. We should have told them. Nothing is worse than a suicide. It leaves everyone with empty questions and self-blame and makes them want to die themselves. There is always hope and love.

Date of Birth

As a society, we find great importance in the age of animate and inanimate objects. Age is something that was made up just to make us forget about the now. Age deceives us from the true value of time.

As an adult meeting a child for the first time, the instant response is, "How old are you?" This gives us predetermined thoughts of whether he or she still believes in Santa or Jesus or understands death. Imagine an attractive, blond-haired, blue-eyed twenty-one-year-old girl. Without thought, your mind reacted with a projected image in your head, and you believed that you knew something about her on a personal level. She could be deaf, dumb, or a blind blonde. Age appears to be more than what meets the eye. Children can never be old enough, and adults can never be young enough.

No one is pleased, and no one will know the age when they die. Trying to reminisce about a past birthday celebration is like trying to recall anything in my life, a haze of confusion. I remember in school, there was this girl who liked me, and I was always good friends with her. She went all out making me this big elaborate card, and everyone signed it.

For my sixteenth, my mom set up a surprise party for me and my friends. Somehow everyone was a good fella and kept their mouth shut. Another year, I sat in my jail cell on lockdown doing absolutely nothing. My cellmate gave me a Twix; it was really nice of him. The most terrifying year, I was brought to the hospital with a head injury; I lost blood from a gash, which had to be stapled closed, and my body also had severe hypothermia. For my twenty-first, I went out with my cousin because I had an earlier birthday than most of my friends. I have always been close with him, and I remember talking to him how scared shitless I was to be a father. Blood is thicker than wine.

I've had the honor to share the date with my godmother, who has always been a guiding light for me. I have even dated a girl with the same birthday as me. I'm terrible with dates and names, so that worked out nicely for me. One year I was enjoying my favorite pastime from the comfort of my home. I received a gift from the Steelers when they announced their linebacker LaMarr Woodley's birthday was the same as mine, year and all.

The best birthday is most definitely always the last. You will never know if you will have the opportunity to celebrate the day of your birth again. Thanks, Mom and Dad; without you, none of this would be possible. Each year, I am proud of myself for surviving another 365 days and nights in this world. We don't give ourselves enough credit for just staying alive in this spinning universe. Congratulations on living. It is not an easy thing to do…or is it? How old am I? Old enough to know better… now but buy me a beer.

Drug Faith

Faith in drugs can strip the world naked and show all the raw truths for the seeker to discover. Spiritual guidance is sought after by people all throughout the world, and Mother Nature will always show the way. If being a whore is the oldest occupation in the world, then drugs have to be the oldest faith. As humans must eat in order to survive, then during our history, we must have consumed everything on earth. We learned what will kill us, nourish us, heal us, and guide us to the light. Certain members of society have devoted their lives to the knowledge of these flowers, plants, fungi, gases, liquids, and animals. These select were known as medicine men, holy men, witches, wise men, doctors, alchemists, gods and goddesses, and as many others before them, were known as drug addicts.

There is a connection between drugs and religion throughout time. As in most religions and spiritual practices, some knowledge are kept secret from the general population because not all can accept the oneness with God. I have complete faith that drugs have shown me the light, the darkness, and all the shades in between.

I know the world does not contain all good people and all bad people and that life is not black and white. We are all capable of doing anything, which may be a blessing or a curse. It is amazing that the body, mind, and soul can survive and thrive through extreme highs and lows in life. I have suffered some of the most horrific tragedies; however, I gratefully accept them because I also have been given miracles in life that I thought were reserved only for God. Everything has a balance, an equilibrium, and a moderation. There are many kinds of faith, and together we all meet at the sun.

Clones' Lives Matter Too

Every cell in our body is replicated and reproduced every seven years. Our body makes millions of cells each day, and we need this adaptation in order to survive a long life. This utterly important cellular communication and replication gives us an idea of why cloning is very valuable.

We like to think that we all are unique and special in the world. In the importance of life of all time, we as humans or individuals are not important at all. Life on earth has been around for millions of years. Evolution has been from the collection of molecules into the collection of cells into the collection of species. From them all, cloning was the cause of creation. The DNA of a tree is made the same as of a human, only the components are in a different order. We all come from the same original organism, which you may call earth or God.

Earth created a DNA structure that was cloned for millions of years; however, over that time, some mutations have occurred, which created new species. Nothing is perfect in life. There is always a chance something could happen. Humans have only been around for a few thousand years, but our lifeblood has been around for millions. We must sexually reproduce in order for our species to continue. We do not call each baby a clone, but from an outside perspective, it is just that. This clone was only replicated to replicate in the future. The strong survive, and the weak die of all the clones.

Somewhere along the timeline, souls played more of a role in life. Souls suddenly make clones into individuals. Clones can have names and numbers and be categorized. Individuals have great bonding among one another, but none matters in the spectrum of life as a whole. Although in one in a million clones of humans, there is a mutation, and this mutation will stand out from the rest.

Special people have been documented all throughout the years, and some were good, and some were evil. Both were viewed in almost the same manner. Not all mutations work, and some take many years for the positive change to take hold. Most mutations do not live long enough to see their great importance to life.

As a clone, you will continue to live on earth forever. Your components will break down over time, but eventually they'll gather again to form a new clone. We all live forever in life; you don't have to wait seven years to change.

SECTION 5

Mind Dreams

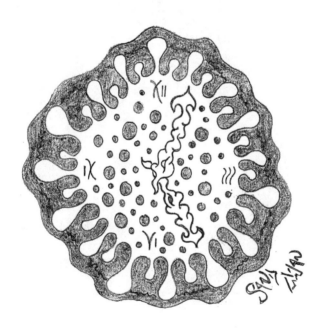

Wonder

I wonder about my dreams more intuitively than my waking life. I see good. I see bad, and there is no control. Faces fade, and laughs follow. I can be anyone I want, but I shall not. I can give you two opposing views, with a million in between, which I can be comfortable enough to function with. I fear myself and what I see. I know I am not evil, but it is intertwined in my eyes. My soul has wandered from my body for many moons. Now it has returned with countless visions of others' lost souls. Many dark days have passed. I have found other ways to catch sight of the light.

Today I Live

I woke up happy today. I didn't roll over and hate life. I can't remember the last time it felt good to get out of bed. When real life can feel as good as the dream world, the possibilities of both dimensions are endless, except the real ones will be remembered in the hearts of others. It is difficult to hold on to this perspective of life, for one step in any direction and it can change. But I must believe that if I can seek beauty, I can find it anywhere and everywhere. Now I don't have to live in the dream realm any longer; I can close my eyes and just imagine what the next day has to offer for me. *Today I love to live and live to love!*

Game of Life

My mind tells me I'm alive; my mind tells me I'm dead. My mind tells me I'm full of grace; my mind tells me I'm full of dread. I've been on a magical journey of mystery, only to awake and realize it was a dream. I have received answers to questions about past memories, only to find out the dream world tricked me yet again.

Why does the mind deceive itself over and over? It seems as if there is a game played by my awake life and my dream life about the validity of truth and what we desire to be true. If I add the two sides together, does that equal the real me or just throw another player into the mix? From time to time, I detect truth from lies in both realms. However, it is easy to forget these findings; and yet again, I'm lost in the world. Fiction and nonfiction, good and evil, yin and yang, I must start with the corner piece to complete the puzzle.

All that is, space and emptiness, where my mind has endless opportunities to play whatever game that is desired. Anything is possible, and everything is questionable. It's up to the third player—the soul—to keep the score.

Black Hole

I closed my eyes and drifted away to this special place that is dark all day. No one can see; no one can hear. Don't be afraid; there is little to fear. I don't want to leave this place; I want to stay. But you will eventually or you'll have to pay. So I open my eyes so I can see. All these weird are people staring at me, so I found a way to hide from the light. It's one hell of a ride, so hold on tight. I can tell you the way if you'd like to go. But it's a one-way ticket to the show. There are plenty of people who have gone there, but choose wisely, beware. Watch your time in this dark place; no one knows where you are without a trace. In this dream world, you can get lost in your mind, so get out of the haze before you are blind.

Bubble

The glimmer of bubbles blinded my eyes, while night fell and the moon began to rise. The blurred doubles laughed all around, but I heard no sound, so my glance drifted toward the ground.

As I raised my head, I could not understand, but Father Time appeared with sand gently flowing through his hand. Suddenly everything stood still all around; everything was stopped, and even the bubbles were bound.

I could now tell the faces were not laughing at all, as tears of sadness stood still in the air and could not fall. The Sand Man slowly shook his head from side to side. I turned to run, but there was nowhere to hide. As I stumbled toward the front of the room, my loved ones were gathered and full of gloom.

I reached for my mother but could not feel. My skin began to crawl and become cold as steel. I looked down at the mirrored figure on the floor and realized that death had knocked on my door. The dark man looked at me with a grin, and I understood my life was full of sin. As the last of his sand hit the ground, my bubble burst without a sound.

Blackout

My head is screaming before I even open my eyes to the new day. I realize that I am not in my own room and I have no idea where I am or where I was the night before. As I get out of bed, I find out that I am completely naked except for my socks. While I dress myself, I question whether I should open the bedroom door, but instead I look out the window to try to locate my position.

I now know that I am across town from where I live, and I am also two stories up from the ground. I reach in my pockets and find three Snickers wrappers, a few bunched-up dollar bills, five lighters, one smoke, and a handful of grass. As I contemplate why this grass was so special to me that I had to tear it from the earth and place it in my pocket, I thoughtlessly light my one cigarette with one of my five lighters.

I feel stuck in the beginning of a dream, with no direction, like the smoke that flows from my dry lips. Softly I start to close my eyes to the mysterious world I have awakened to, and the bedroom doors slam open. As I jump in the air and my grass clippings float to the floor, I see a familiar face that brings relief to my mind. Relief quickly turns to panic as my friend tells me to grab my shoes and run up into the attic. I found out some information about my whereabouts and situation.

I begin to laugh as I slowly understand the endless questions running through my head. I blacked out, and now it's time to connect the puzzle pieces from everyone and attempt to make a picture of the night.

Dreams

I sometimes lose emotions and feelings between the realms of reality. The ecstasy of sleep allures me, sometimes for days at a time. The effects of the awake life are no longer desired because the laws of the dream world are infinite.

Being in touch with myself unfortunately means being out of touch with all. The knowledge that is obtained throughout an entire day can be given in mere minutes in the dream sense.

A power nap can turn into a beautiful novel if given the right moment. I do believe that dreams represent the everyday lives that we live, just from a different perspective.

When I am active in addiction, I dream about getting high and stashing the rest of my stuff under a dresser or something. I would wake up and instantly check for my stuff, only being left with the desire to get high for the rest of the day.

The nightmares of life cannot escape you. I can only imagine what haunts the dreams of serial killers and rapists. I don't know if they would get off or be bothered.

When I live a clean, healthy, awake life, my sleep is much more pleasant. I can feel relaxed enough to go to sleep comfortably and to wake at ease. I do not remember my dreams often but do feel a sense of understanding during my dreams. It feels as if a whole other life exists while I am asleep. This person lives a similar life but has even crazier scenarios, which is hard to believe. It's like being drunk and trying to remember a movie I saw when I was drunk. The story is a little hazy, but I know it's a good movie.

Moderation is a very difficult thing to deal with, especially for an addict. Sleep is as much of a drug to me as anything. I have chosen sleep over everything: sex, drugs, and rock and roll, as well as the other fine things in the awake life such as work, school, and responsibilities. The highs of sleep will never be higher than those of life; however, enjoy searching.

SECTION 6

Higher Love

We Are God

Have you ever felt like a God? The feeling that you are untouchable, not just from man but also from God. Knowing that you can get anything you want without repercussion. Being indulged with anything your heart desires. You will push your limits to the fullest, and you are all in on everything. You can control the will of others and command them to do whatever you please. The feeling of invincibility and the ability to lead others is a very serious disease that affects us all. Like any addiction, we are all vulnerable to this disease.

People will do anything to sustain their godlike feeling. Many people die or have their lives ruined because of these people who think they are gods. Some try to be the god of business, god of government, god of gangs, god of drugs, god of war, god of earth, and god of God. Schools are full of gods as well. There are the popular gods, the athletic gods, the smart gods, the bully gods, and the drug-addicted gods. It is a global disease that no one knows about. It is all about the ego and the control of other egomaniacs. Some people view it as healthy competition.

However, all the gods know the dirty stuff they did to get them where they are. We need to research and educate everyone about this disease. I have a simple plan to help stop the gods. Instead of believing that you are a god, believe that you are God. Not just you but everything has God in it. We are all one God. If we could connect everybody (everything else is already connected), enlightenment will spread through our souls as the nirvana begins. For people who are down and out in life, finding out that they are God will definitely brighten their day. One person's actions throughout the day create a butterfly effect that alters God everywhere. When people can accept that they are part of God, then they can stop listening to the so-called gods.

Balance will be returned to life on earth. God is in all of us; you are God, we are God, and the trees that touch the clouds are definitely God. I know what it feels like to be a God. It has humbled me yet empowered me as well. Most people have their own personal vision of what their God looks like. All you have to do is open your eyes, lift up your heart, and love will keep us together. God is everywhere, and it is up to you to find what you seek. The more God that you can find, the more wisdom you may gain. I am God, and I will help save the world.

Christmas

Everyone loves Christmas, and the exchange of presents makes it all the more enjoyable. As a kid, all you care about is what is under the tree for yourself; although, as you become older, you start to appreciate giving. Personally I have always taken pleasure in giving my heart to others. Material possessions have a finite life span. My cheap gifts can be infinite.

Even as a child, I comforted others and did what I could to help the situation. I was the man of the house, and my mother needed me. A hug has the beautiful ability to make a person feel better than anything in the world. I have witnessed just as many grown men cry as I've seen children. Pain can be felt by your dog even if your wife doesn't notice that something is wrong. People learn to conceal their pain because our society feels you are damaged if you express yourself. They would rather give you a pill instead of talk to you about the issue.

We are conditioned to these views from watching the news, which is a continuous strain of murders, arrests, violence, misfortune, and enough medications to aid the pain. This leaves people terrified of everything and anything, whereas others are desensitized to these daily tragedies. They want us to believe that the end of the world is coming so they can extort whatever they want from us.

The world isn't such an awful place; it is about perspective, and that is the best gift I can offer the universe. If I can aid in your self-perception and you can feel it within, then you will be challenged to view yourself from every angle. At times it is easier for others to understand you better than yourself. It is up to them to help you with the individual care of your perceptions.

I love how people's eyes light up when they understand the gifts I have given them. Over the course of my life, I have met many special people who have assisted in my perception. People come and go, but the gifts collected over time—and if acknowledged—make you continue to grow. Some take time to grow on you, like a sweater you acquired from Santa. Help others if you want to help yourself. Sometimes you need someone to point out the stars and help you see the reflection in the water.

Equilibrium

The perpetual cycle of light and dark will always remain constant, and thus we must, in turn, assist the sequence. There are many forces at work for the light and dark system to function properly. It makes the earth survive and affects how all the mycological dimensions evolve. Some people join forces as if this is a war to be won. The equilibrium of the universe must maintain its balance for survival.

Embrace in the allness of the isness in the power of now. It's like smoke dancing through the sunlight from a window. Observe the light and the dark and bend them into a prism to understand the truth.

Think

I think, therefore I am. The more I think, the less I am. I am not my mind, and my mind is not who I am. I am something greater and more powerful than my mind. I lose sight of what's important when I contemplate this importance. When I see a sunrise, I do not need to think that it is beautiful; it is felt before the thought. My senses help to enhance my feelings, yet they are not my master either. I am able to sense beauty with no stimuli of thought process. From out-of-body experiences come wonder; out-of-mind experiences come feeling and emotion. Both make me look crazy in the eyes of others.

Enlightenment is a fine line in the world we live in. This is something, as humans in the spiritual world, we strive for. It is something that is found with the soul, not the mind or the senses. The soul is my everything and my nothing. It is my connection to the greater and more powerful. I can't control my soul, but I can influence the power. Not being in control is frightening, but once accepted, a freedom is born. It's all about balance; it is something I'm not trying to understand, just feel.

Surround Yourself with Good People

Throughout life, I have chosen to surround myself with others who have been deemed not fit for society. I have also been forced by our fit society to live with the unfit. I am not sure if this is a form of discipline or just separation. People who have been to prison view it as the same as a college education or military service. The more time that someone has in prison, the higher up he will become in the ranks. Criminals don't quit their occupation by being placed behind bars.

Similar to laws in America, the prison system has its own set of made-up and forever-changing laws. Most are set up to devalue the life of an inmate. This just leaves most laws not followed, because an individual needs to believe in laws in order to fully commit themselves. Society fears the creativity of a criminal. Society fears criminals because the criminals have lost belief in society's system. Society can take away its so-called freedoms, but by giving in to society, a criminal must give away their morals.

Society gives the right to say that one person is better than another because of their belief system. Our morals say that we are all equal and no person is better than the next. I've never attacked other people; I have only abused myself. I have aided others my entire life, and I know I am a good person. I don't need society's opinion about me. If helping others in any way, shape, or form is a crime, then send me to the executioner because my beliefs will not change. Father, forgive them, for they know not what they do.

Time

The paradox of our time in history is that we have taller buildings but shorter tempers, wider freeways, but narrow viewpoints. We spend more, but have less; we buy more, but enjoy less. We have bigger houses and smaller families, more conveniences, but less time. We have more degrees but fewer senses, more knowledge, but less judgment, more experts, yet more problems, more medicine, but less wellness.

We drink too much, smoke too much, spend to recklessly, laugh too little, drive too fast, get too angry, stay up too late, get up too tired, read too little, watch TV too much, and pray too seldom. We have multiplied our possessions, but reduced our values. We talk too much, love too seldom, and hate too often.

We've learned how to make a living, but not a life. We've added years to life, not life to years. We've been all the way to the moon and back, but have trouble crossing the street to meet a new neighbor. We conquered outer space but not inner space. We've done larger things, but not better things.

We've cleaned up the air, but polluted the soul. We've conquered the atom, but not our prejudice. We write more but learn less. We plan more, but accomplish less. We learned to rush, but not to wait. We build more computers to hold more information, to produce more copies than ever, but we communicate less and less.

These are the times of fast foods and slow digestion, big men and small character, steep profits and shallow relationships. These are the days of two incomes but more divorce, fancier houses but broken homes. These are the days of quick trips, disposable diapers, throwaway morality, one night stands, overweight bodies, and pills that do everything from cheer, to quiet, to kill. It is a time when there is much in the showroom window and nothing in the stockroom. A time when technology can bring this to you, and a time when you either indulge or ignore.

Unknown Author

SECTION 7

One Love

Love

Love is not true or false
It is not opinion of something you just say
Love has no boundaries or protection
To reach your love, you'll always

The worst thing in the world is not being able to reach the one
you love
If you don't have love, you might as well die
Love may be a lot to work for
Always go for that chance, always try

Love can either make or break you
It is dangerous and difficult to figure out
You will never know it's coming till it's there
Love is what life is all about

Never question love or fake it
Love is real; love is pure
When you find love, hold it tight
Go for the heart, go to the core

Good Old Gram

My heart fills with joy as I become closer and closer to visiting the greatest person in the world. Every time I think of her, all the troubles in my life seem to disappear and all I can do is smile. As I finally reach my destination, I slam the car door, the car that this great person so generously gave me. Even before I enter the house, I can smell the sweet aroma of something baking inside. As I turn the key and even before I can enter the home, I am embraced by an angel. This angel is not the usual blond, skinny, young, beautiful girl. This one is a short, slightly chubby, lovely old lady who melts my heart with her smile. My grandmother tells me that she has missed me oh so much and she is so thankful that I have come to see her. At this point, I, at last, figure out that the sweet smell entering through my nostrils is my one and only favorite, Gram's apple pie.

After hugs and kisses, I am able to take off my coat and shoes to enter this warm and cozy paradise. As with most old people's homes, the house is always a cool eighty degrees. There is the Virgin Mary statue that I repainted and gave new life to, something so precious to my gram, presented honorably in a spotlight. The house is littered with pictures of family members all over the walls and counters. The television is almost deafening with some priest praising the Word of the Lord. As I make my way toward the kitchen, I become engulfed by more heat attempting to retreat like an outnumbered soldier on the battlefield, although this heat is a mild consequence for the amazing party that will take place with my taste buds.

As I sit down and begin the conversation, I can see that my poor old gram is so ecstatic that her favorite grandson has come to join her for the day. I tell her to get a cat to help keep her company and, as a bonus, to rid her of her dreadful fear of mice. However, she insists that she is happy with things the way they are and just says that I should come and live with her instead. She then places the day's newspaper in front of me but never gives me ample time to read with all her excitement involved in the conversation. The biggest concern on her mind is always, What would you like to eat? It doesn't matter if I am hungry or if I just ate, my answer must always please her as she always pleases me. She is the most amazing cook in the world, and over the years, I have become spoiled by her food and lost taste for other people's cooking. We often tease about opening a restaurant together and making millions from her incredible talent.

She is so grateful for her life and shows it with her everyday living. My grandmother was born into an Italian family of twelve siblings, and family has always been the most important thing in her life. This blessed person was born on January 15, 1916, in her family home of Altoona. Her family never had too much because of the difficult years that she was growing up in and also the abundance of children her loving parents had to put up with. She says that she could never be happier with how her life turned out. Gram had a loving husband who enjoyed her cooking and company for most of her life, and she was fortunate to have three children just as beautiful as she, over a dozen grandchildren, and even plenty of great-grandchildren. You can tell her family means a lot to her just by looking at the refrigerator—upon which is draped from head to toe with pictures of us all.

After the incredible meal that has overstuffed us both and an earful that starts to pour out the other ear, it is time to relax. I help to clean up the damage that she has put the kitchen through even though she tells me to let it be. Then I help walk this fragile elderly lady into the living room toward her seat that has become molded to her body over the many years of abuse. She tells me more stories from her past, some of which I have heard before, but I still keep entertained by this angel I call my gram. After we are both pleased with the long conversation, a peaceful silence enters the home for the first time since my arrival. I love to nap on her couch, which has been reupholstered more times than I can count. I spent many days here as a child and as an adult, and this place seems like home to me. A nap is always in order after an overflowing meal and storytime for both of us. As I close my eyes and drift away to a secret, dark, special place, I realize how perfectly at peace of heart, body, and soul I have become. My best friend means everything in the world to me, and I never want to leave. She has given me a gift that has become a part of me, and now I can share it with my own child and hopefully with my grandchildren someday. Who would have ever thought that this little old lady could have so much to offer the world? I wish that we did open the restaurant so she could share her gift with thousands of others; however, like I said, family is most important to her, and she wants to give all she has to the people she loves most.

Love Never Dies

Human beings have the fragility to forget their entire human existence. They cannot remember their religion, their children, their name—anything about their human form. The one thing that will always remain constant in life is love.

Your gram may not know your name, but she knows that you belong and she loves you. Love is found in being. It's sad to watch someone you love lose their memory; however, it is a miracle to realize that they did not lose their love.

We are not humans, and we are not beings. We are human beings. There is more to all of us than what meets the eye. My pap had Alzheimer's and needed hospitalization for his illness. One day he was dying and was rushed to the emergency room. I'm not sure if he knew who I was at that point. I asked him if he needed water or the doctor or this or that. He took my hand and said he needed me.

Withered Rose

One petal at a time. After my pap passed away, I kept a rose from the funeral. It sat on top of my dresser, and I looked at it every day. Over the years, the petals withered away, which made me protect the rose even more. When all the petals fell off, I saved them to decorate one of my pieces of art. I took care of my rose; I loved my rose. Then suddenly one day, my house caught fire, and my rose was taken from me too. My rose would always be close to my heart, but I understood it was okay to let it go.

Say hi to my buddy, Uncle Ray. I will always love and miss you, Aunt Theresa.

Forever Friends

Competition and pride in life can be created out of flowers and weeds. Have you ever cut your grass and halfway before you are done, your neighbor decides to cut his lawn as well, but he has a riding mower? These little things in life make me smile. My gram has taken great care and pride in her rose garden. She says the roses are for the Virgin Mary, but I'm sure Gram has some friendly competitive spirit with her neighbors.

Clete, a competitor on the street, was just laid to rest with roses. He was not a relative; however, I would knock on his front door for trick or treat and would watch ball games with him. He was better than a relative. Over the years, I've done some yard work for the man, and he reminded me every time not to touch the roses. Gram says that his mother treated her like one of her own, and if you're good in Gram's eye, you're good in any eye. Clete lived with his mother until she died at one hundred years of age. And she was laid to the roses herself. I know Mrs. Stalter had twenty years of new jokes saved up for her son to hear.

Gram is now 101 and has outlived most of her roses. Roses have connections all throughout my life, and they all make me smile. This rose is for you, old friend. I tried to pick it through the weeds.

A Piece of Me Will Always Be With You

You will never be alone. Wherever you go, there will always be a piece of me with you and you will always be with me. I dream of us together making apple pies and eating baby carrots from Pap's garden.

All the prayers you have said for me have worked wonders. I do have God in my life. I feel the Holy Spirit stronger than I realize. And I know that I am a child of God. I honestly can say that I can overcome anything that life challenges me with.

Speak of the truth with those who search for it and of knowledge to those who have committed a sin in their error. Make firm the foot of those who have stumbled. Give rest to those who are weary, raise those who wish to rise, and awaken those who sleep.

SECTION 8

Soul Love

Redemption

I forgive you for all your sins and fears that have destroyed your life. You have tormented and invaded the hearts of everyone you touched. Ocean of tears have been wept in your world of pain. You are the poster child for "that would never happen to me." You don't understand why you broke all the laws of God and man and don't understand why you have run from the Master's plan. You question if you should follow your head or your heart, but listen to neither. You ask to be saved, but don't reach out to the arms around you.

Faith comes from those who believe. Belief comes from those who search. Search comes from those who question. You must find the strength in your mind and soul to find your solution to the meaning of life. You must take the weight of the world off your shoulders and offer it to the One larger than yourself. Forgiveness will come if acceptance of punishment is understood and never forgotten. You have the power to create, destroy, and touch the lives of others; however, you can't successfully use this power from God without starting with yourself.

I am allowing this to be done, I am allowing this to be felt, and I am allowing you to be redeemed from the ghosts of your past, present, and future. Now you have the ability to continue from a blank canvas to create a beautiful story. Don't forget the lessons you've been taught from the past, and always welcome open doors in the future. For the present, you are granted the power from God to create a masterpiece.

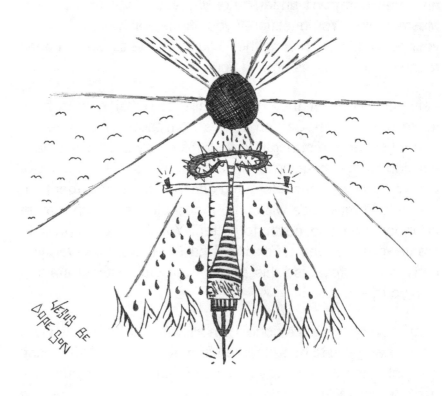

Sky

Some days I cry because I want to die,
But I realize I can fly high in the sky.

Man is more than just flesh and bones.
We are individuals and are not drones.

The human mind will consume the whole feast.
So be aware how to control the beast.

The beat of the heart brings the dance of love.
It glides through the sky like a dove from above.

The soul is what defines the clock of life.
It's found in the eyes and is sharp as a knife.

Light

I opened my eyes, and I could see people staring at me. I tried to run. I tried to hide; but once you see the truth, you cannot see the truth. I have the heart of a lion and the eye of a tiger; I can see in the dark, but the light is clearer. I came, I saw, I conquered; I am as wise as a serpent but as gentle as a dove. The light shines from above to those who love. "Eat, drink, and be merry for tomorrow we die." There is no lie in his eye, so say goodbye to those who don't try. Embrace yourself in the moment, for it has come. Shed a tear, for your fear is here, so hold on, dear. Godspeed, my son, for it has come.

Crown

My journey to recovery will be difficult to bear, but I accepted this challenge, so, devil, beware. One step in front of the other like a baby's first stumble. I got my game face on. I'm ready to rumble.

In order to succeed, I must bleed away all my greed. This is something I need to truly believe indeed. I must forgive the past for treating me with much harm. I broke many hearts with my fake charm. My father abandoned me when I was young. It hurts so bad; it makes me feel numb. But we will meet again someday. I know that it will come.

I must avoid people, places, and things. By cutting loose in life, I'm no longer a puppet with strings. I must give my best friend and lover to another man. And I must understand this is God's demand.

I now have a new family that can truly relate. This choice in life is easy; there will be no debate. I have seen the gates of hell and the trapped souls. I now have a new set of rules, so peace out to you fools. I was lost but now am found. This is something profound that I must lay down my crown before I'm in the ground.

Wisdom

Don't trust all, but desire to know all. There is good in all there is; one just has to know how to go about looking. The eye deceives, but the heart will show the way. Approach cautiously, for respect is power. Enlightenment will open the soul to the balance of life. All is within the strength of the light. Be gentle with open hands, for the warmth will embrace your spirit.

Innocent Soul

Open your eyes so you can see.
Let it go and let it be.

The world is yours for the taking.
Drop the mask; you're not faking.

Breathe in the yin and the yang.
Exhale the blood at the bang.

The spirits run wild in the breeze.
The chains are broken from the disease.

You are no more guilty to your mind.
Freedom is here for you to find.

Wipe away your tears and fears.
Shut your mouth and open your ears.

The best in life is always free.
Just open your heart and you will see.

Wings

The wings gently wrap around my soul;
It glitters softly like a jewel.

As the beat increases at the show,
I am lost and don't even know.

The warmth is felt all around.
The spirit is free and never bound.

Music dances through our eyes.
Truth flows and never dies.

I have risen up to kiss the sky.
Now I'm alive and can never die.

Dual Diagnosis Dilemma

The most frustrating types of illness are the ones that you believe that you don't have control over. When you have to convince others how sick you are or when others have to convince you how sick you have become. It will always be a debate whether mental health and substance abuse issues are true diseases. Most people believe that these problems are made up in the mind and can be solved by choice. They think that problems are only for the weak-minded and not major concerns for the general public.

We can all understand the concepts of the diseases because we have all overeaten or overexercised at some time and become sick and sore from abuse. Even by mourning the death of a loved one. Maybe you were just really excited and anxious about your life. Now imagine those physical and mental situations being a more forceful experience every single day of life—enough to make you want to kill yourself and wish death would take your soul because you are suffering so much. This sounds like an exaggeration to those who don't understand, but it is the truth.

People are capable of understanding things without honestly believing them. People may believe in things without exactly understanding them. And some people have the astonishing capability to achieve both. There is not enough education about these diseases, and people just make it up as it goes along. This creates a genuine dilemma of division, and a solution becomes quickly forgotten. People like to appear that they really care for those in recovery, and yet the same compassionate citizens will turn away from their loved ones who are actively experiencing the disease. The general public turns their back whenever an affected human being needs them the most. And so does the person living the chaos.

Patients who live with dual diagnosis must accept their diseases and rise to the challenge of surviving a quality life. Some patients can overcome acute mental health problems and short-term addiction, which can promote a healthy life without recurring incidents. However, the others who remain chronic will have to endure their own personal situations for the remaining days of their lives. The diseases have the ability to flow in and out of remission, which causes the patients to believe they are back in control. Patients must first be required to believe that they do indeed have a disease. Then the patients must be educated and accumulate all the knowledge possible about their disease. Next the patients have the overwhelming duty to get their loved ones to not only believe but also to understand the diseases.

Keep in mind that the patients need to accept their life-threatening disease and be grateful for the unique gifts that are reserved for them. Most patients repeat this process thousands of times before they are gifted enough to embrace the thorn. Not all addicts have mental problems, and not all mental health patients have addiction issues, although both serpents intertwine with each other. Mental health patients eventually attempt to self-medicate themselves in order to feel like a normal person. Many substance-abuse addicts suffer from both neurological and emotional deficiencies because of heavy drug abuse.

It is complicated to keep both sides of the coin in remission at the same time. The ability to survive each day with these diseases is always a miracle, but all the patient just really wants is for people to believe in them.

Acknowledgments

Justin and I would like to graciously thank the beautiful people who gave inspiration to his vision—God sent angels who gave their time, their support, their skills, and most importantly, their love. Justin's goal and ours is to reach out into hearts and give some understanding and hope to all living with addiction and mental health illnesses. Our angels are Amy Adams, Lisa Georgiana, LuAnne Mencl, Christine O'Conner, Janet Schachtner, and Sharon Slack...also Emily McConnell, EM's Graphic Studio. We are *one love*.

CPSIA information can be obtained
at www.ICGtesting.com
Printed in the USA
LVHW041159171120
671900LV00006B/513